A Surprise at the Farm

Carlos M. Valverde

Published by Coffee Seed Books® LLC,
USA, Arlington, WA 98223
www.coffeeseedbooks.com
Toll free: 1(800) 268-7014

A Surprise at the Farm
Copyright © 2012 Carlos M. Valverde
All rights reserved. No part of this publication may be reproduced, stored in a retrieval system, or transmitted, in any form or by any means, electronic, mechanical, photocopying, recording, or otherwise, without the written prior permission of the author.

Written and illustrated by: Carlos M. Valverde
Colored by: Alicia Kuppler.
Designed by: Cristina Masterjohn. Edited by: Matthew Kelsey

Library of Congress Control Number: 2018910385
A Surprise at the Farm/ Valverde, Carlos M.
Coffee Seed Books® Publishing 5/30/2021
Created in the United State of America.

ISBN: 978-1-943718-15-3 (HC). 978-1-943718-08-5 (SC). 978-1-943718-09-2 (e-book)

This book was originally published by Trafford® Publishing in 2013.
Coffee Seed Books® revision 5/30/2021

Thank you to everyone involved in creating this book!

For Galilea, Camila and Natalia. —CMV

This story happened on a farm where many animals lived, among them a sheep named **Curls.**

Every morning, after breakfast, Curls and her friends went to work.

Each animal had an important job to do

on the farm.

Every evening, after those jobs were done,

Curls and her friends gathered around a fire to talk and rest.

One day, the cow went to visit each of the animals while they were at work. The cow told everyone a secret.

That evening, no one went to the fire except for Curls.

She thought it was strange that her friends weren't there, so she set out to look for them.

When Curls approached the barn she heard **whispering inside.**

She peeked inside the barn through a gap in the door and saw her friends talking quietly. *"How strange!"* she thought.

She was very curious. She wanted to know what her friends were talking about and why she was not invited.

When her friends came out of the barn, Curls acted like she did not know anything about the meeting.

The other animals **did the same.**

She felt sad and thought, "My friends are hiding something from me!"

The mysterious behavior of her friends continued, and she was convinced that her friends

did not like her anymore.

She worried herself SO MUCH that she could not eat or sleep.

A couple of days later, Curls saw that her friends were gathering in the barn like they were going to have a party.

This time, though, they did not hide from her. "Are they going to have a party without me?" she wondered.

Curls felt sad, but also really, REALLY MAD.

"That's enough!" she thought.

"I am leaving this farm today, but first I will tell them that I don't want to be their friend."

When she got to the barn, she pushed the door open and yelled...

"I don't want to be your—"

"Happy birthday!" yelled all her friends as they ran to hug her.

Curls was surprised, and very happy that she was wrong about her friends.

Her friends had been planning a surprise birthday party for her **all this time!**

Curls had not remembered that it was her birthday because she was too busy thinking her friends did not like her.

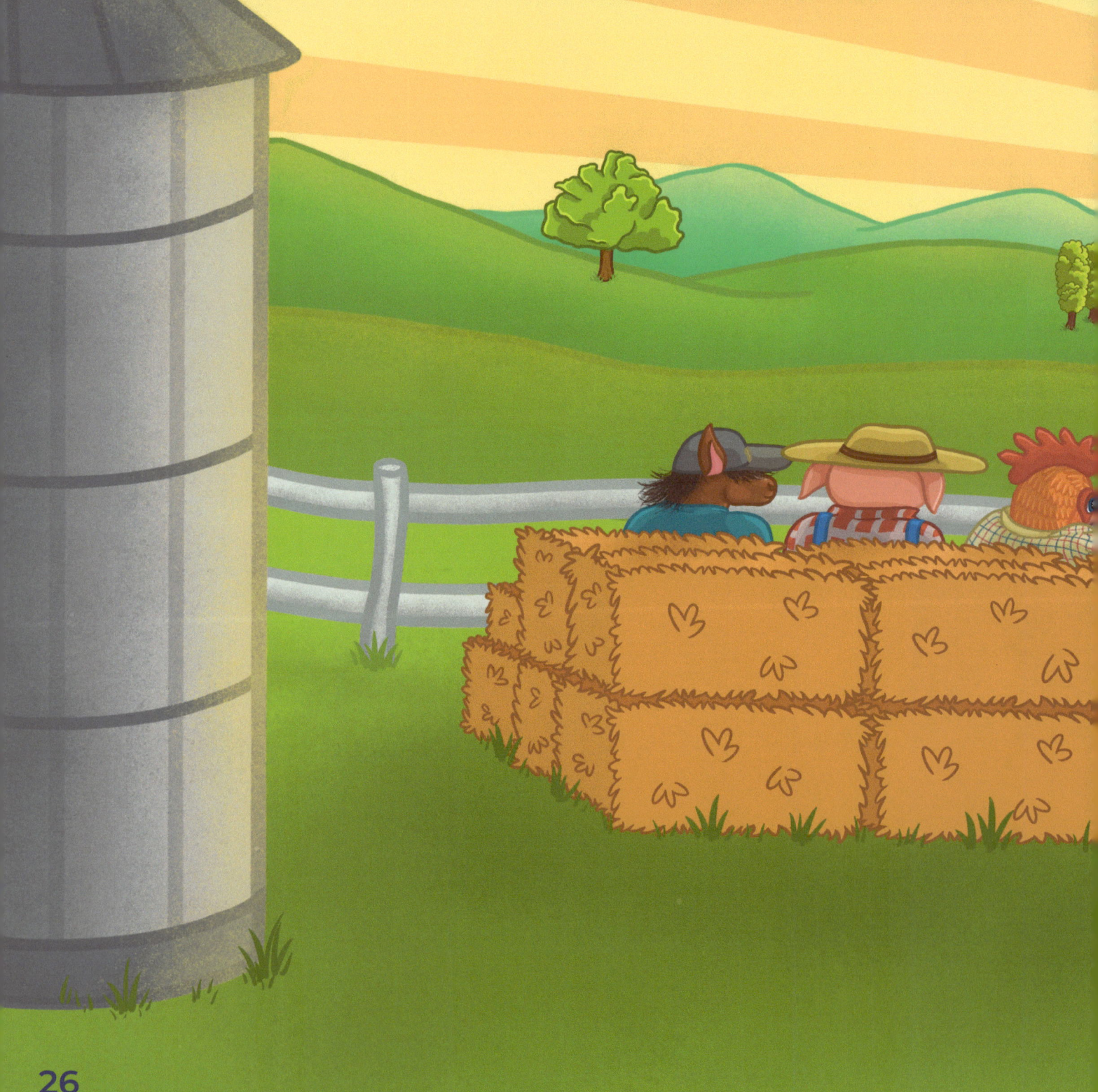

Curls was grateful and happy,

and apologized to her friends for doubting their friendship.

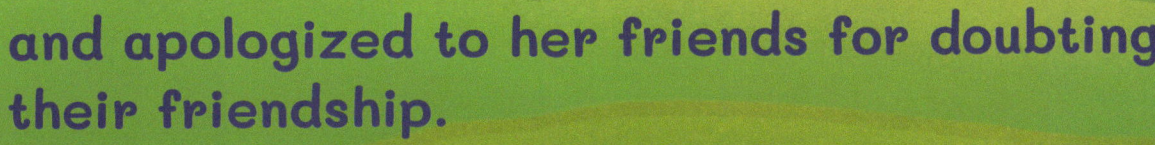

Discussion Ideas

1. Discuss with your children the moral of the story.

2. Ask your child if he or she has ever felt like Curls.

3. Discuss what the child can do if he or she ever feels left out.

Please share your opinion about this book on your favorite social media platform or book retailer website. Thank you!

Other Books By This Author

The Gift

The Grumpy Frog

The Land of Shapes

The Land of Colors

Are You a Mixed-Race Human?

These titles are also available in Spanish and bilingual versions.

www.ingramcontent.com/pod-product-compliance
Lightning Source LLC
Chambersburg PA
CBHW041502220426
43661CB00016B/1224